NORTHWEST NO

A Cradle for British Agriculture, Pol

INTRODUCTION

The northwest corner of Norfolk is a very important agricultural region; with a large-scale arable and grassland landscape and some areas of mixed farming, where pigs and sheep comprise the dominant livestock. With no heavy industry, what little industrial activity exists in the region is mostly concerned with food production; although King's Lynn boasts an extensive paper-making plant and offshore energy production is finding a new future in wind turbine electricity generation.

This very open, rolling countryside is accentuated by the large geometric field patterns of the 18th century bounded by hawthorn hedges and mature oak and beech trees. Frequently offering long views, these rectangular fields are interspersed with significant belts of mixed woodland and plantations, and some remnant heath on the Sandringham Sand Formation in the west. Smaller scale, more intimate pastoral vistas may be found within the several river valleys which drain westwards into The Wash and northwards to the North Sea.

With myriad evidence of Neolithic, Bronze Age, Iron Age, Roman and Anglo-Saxon occupation, here is a region which was exploited, and defended, by the earliest farmers of Britain. But the landscape that we see today was largely created by forward-thinking 17th and 18th century innovative yeomen farmers, who in enclosing their lands oversaw the change from medieval manorial strip farming tended by serf labour, to the modern independently-run agronomy of the 21st century.

But this is also a region of large, landed-gentry estates and magnificent country houses. Leading this change to a modern agricultural economy, and indeed to our modern political system, were three sons of northwest Norfolk, who having profited from their inheritances were determined to improve their lands and lives for the benefit of their own families, and many others. Even today their work lies at the heart of this region, a temperate area blessed by a benign geology and ambient topography which essentially provided the fertile cradle for their pioneering work to prosper.

TOPOGRAPHY

The northwest region of Norfolk principally lies on the western half of a plateau of rolling farmland of glacial sands termed the 'Good Sands'. These fertile loams gently slope eastward towards the 'High Claylands' of central Norfolk. The region is bounded northwards by the waters of the North Sea, whilst to the west the

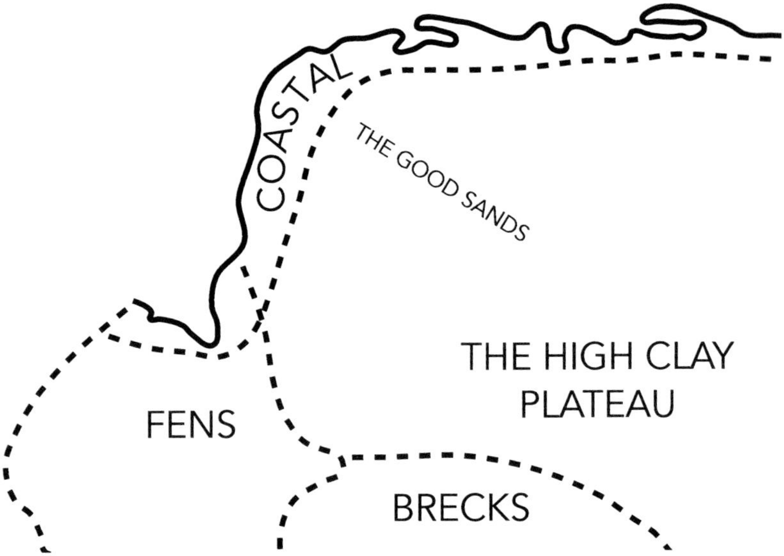

Map showing northwest Norfolk's different regions.

'Good Sands' give way to lower lying claylands and peat Fens skirting The Wash. The main A47 trunk road largely provides the southern boundary of the region dividing it from the rich low-lying fens of Marshland to the south and west, which extend to the county border with Lincolnshire at Sutton Bridge. To the south and east lie the poorly productive sands of Breckland, one of the driest parts of the country. Northwest Norfolk however, with its adjacent North Sea coast, benefits from a temperate climate sufficient to sustain arable agriculture and support its many small rivers. These unique, spring-fed streams rise from the low but distinctive chalk ridge running north-south lying towards the eastern side of the region. The region's principal river, the Great Ouse, flowing northward into the Wash, drains an enormous watershed from the Midlands, which today provides a considerable flow of water to northwest Norfolk, and in times past was an essential means of communication to and from the heart of England. Similarly, the river Nene, running from the Midlands through Peterborough and Wisbech, pours into The Wash at Sutton Bridge lying on the region's western boundary.

The undisputed capital of the region with a population of 43,000 is the ancient port of King's Lynn, with the other principal coastal communities comprising the seaside resort of Hunstanton, seventeen miles [27kms] to the north, and the smaller port of Wells-next-the-Sea lying some thirty miles [48 kms] to the east. Whilst both ports have a long fishing tradition, today their much-reduced fleets are mainly concerned with catching shrimps, cockles and other shellfish. Most of this coastline remains undeveloped and is designated an 'Area of Outstanding Beauty' [AONB] hosting a string of nature reserves from Heacham to Wells and beyond. These include RSPB Titchwell, RSPB Snettisham and Norfolk Wildlife Trust [NWT] reserves at Holme Dunes, Holkham, Scolt Head Island and Cley Marshes.

The market town of Fakenham, with its renowned Fakenham Racecourse, is home to some 11,000 souls and lies twenty five miles [40kms] inland from the coast in the centre of the region; whilst the smaller market town of Swaffham, with a population of 7,300, is on the region's southern boundary. In between the visitor will find numerous smaller villages, often set around a village green with a large pond, with all of these communities ever dependent on the all-prevailing agricultural activity of the region, although today tourism also forms an increasingly important sector of the region's economy.

GEOLOGY

As a dominantly agricultural county all of Norfolk's various regions are defined by the nature of the soils which supports this agriculture, and these in turn are dictated by the underlying geology. Norfolk's oldest rocks of Upper Jurassic and Lower Cretaceous age are found here in the west, comprising a series of clays, sands and sandstones. In the far west bordering Lincolnshire the flat fields of peat are underlain by Kimmeridge Clay of Upper Jurassic age and these are superseded eastwards by north-south running Lower Cretaceous strata. These comprise the Sandringham Sand Formation, containing a commercially important Leziate Member of fine-grained quartzite, used to build the Roman *Branodunum* Shore Fort at Brancaster, with the stone later re-purposed and used in at least six local churches. The facing stone of Castle Rising is in this quartzite, and it's also found in dwellings and farm buildings, especially in the villages of Ringstead and Wormegay. Today, the Leziate quarry supplies many tons of these fine-grained sands for glassmaking and fracking. Overlying this is the Dersingham Formation of Small Carr ferruginous sandstone, in turn overlain by the much thicker

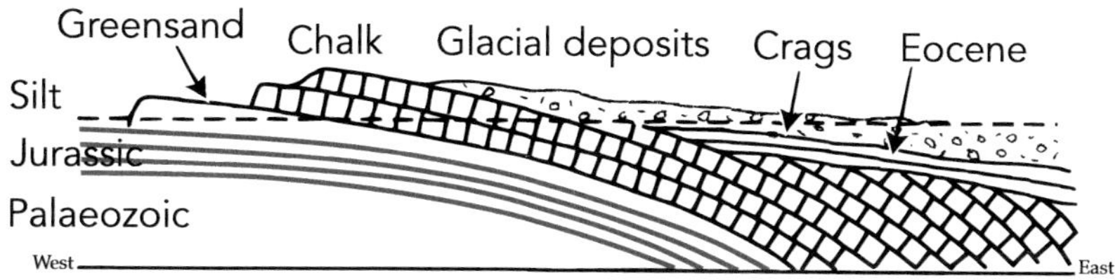

Cross-section showing the underlying geological strata of Norfolk, west to east.

Carrstone Formation which provides the distinctive gingery Big Carr, used as building stone for the so-called 'gingerbread houses' found all across the western part of the region.

At the boundary of the Lower and Upper Cretaceous lies a narrow band of Gault Clay, which in the north of the region is overlain by the equally narrow Hunstanton Formation; revealed at the coast in the spectacular and unique Red Chalk at the base of Hunstanton Cliffs. Above this comes the Lower Chalk of the Upper Cretaceous, named the Grey Chalk containing fossil horizons of the large bivalve *Inoceramus,* together with brachiopods, ammonites, echinoids and even fish bones and teeth. There is no need to climb the cliffs to find these specimens; close examination of the fallen boulders at the base of the cliff at low tide will reveal all these species to the keen-eyed observer. The chalk often contains firmer horizons of 'clunch', with blocks of this material used as distinctive building stone mainly in the east of the region.

The extensive outcrop of the White Chalk subgroup, comprising the Upper and Middle chalk, forms a shallow escarpment sloping west to east containing important aquifers, separated from the coastal strip by a distinctive scarp slope. The Upper Chalk is not revealed in Hunstanton cliffs; apart from an occasional small quarry it is difficult to find any evidence of this vast chalk outcrop, although it extends well beyond the region right across Norfolk to Norwich and beyond. This is because eastwards the chalk is blanketed by superficial deposits of Boulder Clay, plastered onto the landscape by the glaciers of the Pleistocene age.

The Dinosaur Coprolite Rush

The discovery in 1874 of extensive coprolite deposits between West Dereham and Downham Market proved to be highly significant in the development of agriculture in northwest Norfolk, and also promoted trade in the port of King's Lynn. Coprolites are the fossil remains of mainly marine dinosaurs such as pliosaurs and plesiosaurs; often found as fossil dung from these creatures, but more commonly as concretions of their heavily mineralised bones and teeth. These dung and bone nodules were formed in Lower Cretaceous times by wave action in a narrow sinuous seaway stretching from The Wash to the Isle of Wight, and were subsequently buried in the Gault Clay which formed as the sea deepened.

Coprolites with many small inclusions. One has a complete toe bone from a small deer called a leptomeryx. Found in northwest Nebraska.

Most significantly, these fossils

contained phosphates, which in the 1840s industrial chemists had shown were most important in stimulating plant growth, particularly if the material was treated with sulphuric acid to form superphosphate. Up to that time lime marl and animal dung had traditionally been used to fertilise the land, but dung was relatively low in phosphates and marl slow to release its calcium phosphate to good effect. However the mineral could be obtained from bones ground into bone meal which provided the first artificial fertilizers, although bonemeal was also slow acting. Fossil coprolites provided a much better source, and by the 1870s an important and lucrative artificial fertilizer industry had developed in Suffolk and Bedfordshire, with these Norfolk deposits representing the most northern part of this industry. Local landowners made considerable fortunes from the coprolite workings, where the nodules were dug out by teams of workers systematically digging trenches across the fields and back-filling them, thus quickly returning the land to agriculture. Although arduous, this work was financially more rewarding and reliable than agricultural labouring, leading to local inflation when farmers had to increase wages to stop the drift to the diggings. A fossil digger's song '*Coprolite Digging Forever*' boldly proclaimed,

'We are jolly young fellows, that do not work fear,
We can work at the fossils; have a pot of good beer,
With our spades and pickaxe, we've no work to seek,
We won't work for farmers for ten bob a week.'

Having been washed and sorted the material was then shipped to the West Norfolk Manure Company established in King's Lynn in 1873, which supplied markets at home and abroad. Artificial fertilizers proved to be essential in boosting agricultural production and providing food for the burgeoning population of Victorian England, with northwest Norfolk shipping its produce to the rapidly growing industrial cities of the Midlands and beyond. However, the passing of the Free Trade Act in the 1870s meant cheap imports from overseas of both food and fertilizers threatened farmers all across Norfolk, causing a widespread slump in agriculture and, by the turn of the century, the coprolite rush was over.

HORDES AND HOARDS

Following the end of the Ice Age, some 10,000 years ago, there is ample evidence that northwest Norfolk was soon occupied by any number of groups of people; Neolithic farmers, Bronze Age and Iron Age settlers, Roman occupiers, Anglo-Saxon tribes and Vikings in their longboats. These hordes of people tilled the land, built forts and roads, buried their dead and most remarkably hid their treasures in hoards, and fortunately for us all too often never returned to retrieve them.

Seahenge

This enigmatic Bronze Age site comprises a circle of fifty-five wooden posts with a massive central stump of an upturned tree root. Originally two-metres high the posts were scientifically dated to 2049BC, with the site located at that time in marshy ground a few kilometres from the sea. Officially named Holme I, there is another double circle of older wooden posts, Holme II, just 100 metres away. Recent research has suggested that Holme I was about commemorating the dead, whilst Holme II was probably part of a burial mound. Holme I has been removed and is now on display in King's Lynn Museum, and although nothing can now be seen of either circle on this vast open foreshore under wide skies, what better place can there be to ponder the intentions of those ancient Norfolk inhabitants all those years ago?

Holme I.

Snettisham Treasure Hoards

The Snettisham gold hoards, discovered between 1948 and 1990, form the richest Iron Age treasure ever discovered in this country, comprising gold and silver torcs, bracelets, coins and metal ingots. Some 175 gold torcs have been recovered, either made of multiple strands of intricately twisted precious metal or curved hollow cylinders of gold; both were designed to be worn around the neck. The coins were used to date the hoards at around 70BC, but curiously, to date, no

The Snettisham Hoard.

buildings or workshops of a comparable age have been discovered nearby. Many of the torcs were old or broken, suggesting that these were workshop hoards, buried for safe keeping to be later retrieved and turned into new jewellery. Snettisham church hosts a comprehensive display telling the story of the treasure hoards, with the objects themselves on display at the British Museum and Norwich Castle Museum. Gold torcs are not found in other parts of Norfolk; it could be that people living in this region were able to obtain large quantities of gold by controlling the flow of North Sea trade in and out of The Wash. Perhaps the legend of the Pedlar of Swaffham and his treasure hints of a long tradition of such discoveries in northwest Norfolk.

The Sedgeford Hoard

Just three miles from Snettisham another torc was discovered at Sedgeford in 1965, remarkably a missing piece of this torc was found in 2004 by members of the Sedgeford Historical and Archaeological Research Project [SHARP]. Started in 1996, this long running research and training project has attracted volunteer archaeologists from all over the country to its summer digs, with some remarkable finds being made. Most notably, in 2003 the Sedgeford Hoard of Iron Age Gallo-Belgic gold staters [coins] stuffed into a large cow bone was discovered, and on the same day an Iron Age horse burial. The project has also investigated the 'Boneyard', an extensive Anglo-Saxon cemetery and nearby settlement, a late Neolithic/early Bronze Age crouched burial and a middle Iron Age crouched burial. All this clearly demonstrates that Sedgeford has been an important settlement and agricultural community since the first farmers cleared the land some 6000 years ago. Sedgeford church hosts SHARP meetings and here you will also find much information about the project.

Iron Age Forts

Northwest Norfolk is also distinguished by circular or oval banked enclosures of Iron Age Forts, with a cluster in the north of the region at Warham, Holkham and South Creake, and a single example further south at Narborough. This fort is also associated with a long embankment, the Bicham Ditch. Usually known as 'hillforts', only the Bloodgate Fort at South Creake is on a hilltop, all the others are located in river valleys, or in Holkham's case surrounded by coastal marshes. Both Warham and Bloodgate forts are open access sites, Holkham Fort is in the

Holkham National Nature Reserve and best viewed from their bird hide. Much speculation to the purpose of these forts as defensive enclosures, settlements, trading centres or religious sites continues to rage, but whatever their use they remain as upstanding reminders that this bounteous region supported numerous diverse communities prior to the Roman invasion.

Roman Occupation

The Roman occupation of northwest Norfolk was all about using the fertile soils to grow large quantities of grain, and installing the necessary infrastructure to readily supply their Continental armies. The region is crossed by two major Roman roads; Peddars Way heads northwards to Holme next the Sea, whilst the Denver to Brampton road runs east-west with the Roman towns of Fincham, Narborough and Kempstone lying on its route. A side branch of the Peddars Way gave access to the Roman Shore Fort and port [*Branodunum*] at Brancaster. Roman coin hoards, villas and farms are found scattered across the region, with notable clusters of metalworking sites at Walsingham and Snettisham, and also evidence of temples at both these locations.

Brancaster, 2005.

The Binham Anglo-Saxon Bracteate Hoard

Evidence that northwest Norfolk was an important international 6th century Anglo-Saxon centre comes from the discovery over a number of years in the early 21st century of a significant bracteate hoard found in a field in Binham. These flat, single-sided gold pendants were often fashioned from old Roman coins and show human and animal figures in distinctive designs, perhaps representing Anglo-Saxon gods such as Wodin. Together with bracelets and other finds, these Binham examples compare favourably with similar ritual objects discovered in Germany and Scandinavia, showing clear links with other high status Anglo-Saxon communities. It seems that Binham was an important cultural and religious centre over many centuries culminating in the building of medieval Binham Priory. Some of the hoard is on display at Norwich Castle Museum.

Viking Settlement

The presence of three types of Viking objects, Trefoil Brooches, Scandinavian-type weights and a Thor Hammer Pendant, provides evidence of particularly early

Scandinavian influence in northwest Norfolk. Examples of 9th century Trefoil Brooches, based on Carolingian harness mounts have been found in settlements on the Stiffkey, Burn and Heacham rivers, whilst an exceedingly rare Thor's Hammer Pendant was found by the Babingley river. The wearers of these ornaments may not have been Vikings, but second generation migrants or even Anglo-Saxons pursuing Scandinavian fashion. Finds of Scandinavian-type weights, used for trading, are scattered across the region, with all these objects providing evidence of a cultural force which lasted here for nearly 200 years.

Grimston Ware Pottery

Lying a few miles west of King's Lynn the village of Grimston, and unsurprisingly the nearby hamlet of Pott Row, produced distinctive jug pottery from late Saxon through medieval times. The locally-obtained clay fired to a dark-blue grey with a 'sandpaper' finish, and was usually green-glazed, often with applied faces of bearded men. The pottery was exported all over East Anglia, and through King's Lynn to Scandinavia. Production ceased during the 14th century.

THREE PIONEERS OF EARLY-MODERN BRITAIN

During the 17th and 18th centuries the northwest region of Norfolk produced three pioneers of early-modern Britain who not only exercised their considerable skills in the field of politics, but are also recognised as innovative agricultural reformers. Through their ideas and experimentation these three men laid the foundations of modern agriculture, and as we have seen they were blessed with a remarkably fertile region on which to base their reforms. Their estates were set in a prosperous Norfolk which for centuries had benefitted from well-established communications by sea with both London and the near Continent. But, as the feudal manorial system faded, hastened by the English Civil War and the Glorious Revolution of William and Mary, the time was right for both political and economic change, and these three sons of northwest Norfolk lit the torch of what was to become the Agrarian Revolution.

Robert Walpole 1st Earl of Oxford

Sir Robert Walpole, [1676-1745] of Houghton Hall was the first statesman to be recognised as Prime Minister, in control of the Government for twenty-one years, longer than anyone else. Generally regarded as one of the greatest politicians in British history he was born at Houghton, which lies between Fakenham and King's Lynn. His father was MP for Castle Rising and Robert was elected MP for King's Lynn for his entire political career. Walpole considerably enlarged his country seat and filled it with fine furniture and works of the old masters, most of which can still be admired today by the Hall's many visitors during the summer months.

2nd Viscount Charles Townshend

Statesman and farmer 'Turnip' Townshend [1674-1738] inherited a large estate at East Raynham in Norfolk; Raynham Hall lies a few miles southwest of Fakenham. He was a champion of progressive farming promoting the four-course system involving rotation of turnips, barley, clover and wheat crops. Using turnips as winter feed meant that cattle no longer needed to be slaughtered in October, but could be kept in specially designed cattle sheds, with their valuable manure collected and used to fertilise the land. In this way Townshend not only enhanced much needed agricultural productivity in the face of a rising population, his innovations transformed the face of the Norfolk countryside, with much of this built heritage of farm buildings and yards still apparent today. All this came towards the end of his glittering political career which saw him skilfully directing Britain's foreign policy through the changeover from the Stuarts to the Hanoverian accession. Started in 1619 as a grand country house, Raynham Hall was much embellished a century later by William Kent [1685-1748], today it is occasionally open to the public for special events.

Thomas William Coke, 1st Earl of Leicester

Thomas Coke [1754-1842] of Holkham Hall, generally known as 'Coke of Holkham', not only maintained a long parliamentary career, representing Norfolk or Derby for some fifty-six years; he was also a caring and popular agricultural reformer. Whilst Townshend invented the four-course rotation, Coke made it widely popular. Insisting that his tenants at Holkham pursued the system, he also worked with them, earning their respect by introducing better breeds of sheep and cattle. A memorial to him and his work was erected by public subscription in Holkham Park illustrating his successes, with a Devon longhorn bull, a Southdown sheep, a seed drill and an innovative irrigation scheme. He is buried in Tittleshall St. Mary the Virgin church. Today, Holkham Hall, an elegant 18th century Palladian mansion, sits in a 25,000 acre estate which also includes the foreshore, with the house, park and beach open to visitors during the summer months.

SANDRINGHAM HOUSE AND ESTATE

In 1862 Queen Victoria and husband Prince Albert purchased Sandringham House for £220,000 as a country retreat for their eldest son Albert Edward, Prince of Wales, [1841-1910] in the hope that his somewhat wayward London lifestyle might be moderated with a fine county seat in quiet corner of Norfolk. Albert Edward quickly fell in love with Sandringham and its vast estate, although it didn't do much to curb his louche lifestyle. In the ensuing decades he completely rebuilt the house in what architectural historian Pevsner described as a '*frenetic*

Jacobean' style. The Prince also developed the 8,000 acre estate creating one of the finest shoots in England. When in residence he had all the clocks set forward by half an hour to 'Sandringham time' to give more daylight hours for shooting. Having succeeded his mother in 1902 as Edward VII, he fell ill at Sandringham and died in London in 1910. His son George V [1865-1936] inherited Sandringham and was even more enamoured of the place than his father, describing it as '*dear old Sandringham, the place I love better than anywhere else in the world*'. He revelled in all manner of country pursuits including shooting and breeding race horses, one of which he named '*Anmer*' after the estate village. It was with '*Anmer*' that Suffragette Emily Davison had her fatal encounter on Derby Day in June 1913. George was married to Queen Mary of Teck, [1867-1953] and most of their children, including two future kings, were born at York Cottage on the estate. Their youngest son Prince John [1905-1919] lived all of his short troubled life at Sandringham. Despite his epilepsy John frequently played with the children of estate workers; his charming letters once featured on the BBC Antiques Roadshow and clearly showed that he both wrote and spoke in the Norfolk dialect.

A Right Royal Christmas

George V made the first royal Christmas broadcast from Sandringham House in 1932, and it was here that he died in 1936, to be succeeded by his eldest son Edward VIII, who inherited Sandringham as the private property of his father. After the abdication George VI bought Sandringham from his elder brother, and he too was devoted to the House, writing to his mother; '*I have always been so happy here...*' George VI died at Sandringham on February 6th 1952, his coffin rested in St. Mary Magdalene Church for two days before lying in State at Westminster Hall, London. In succeeding him his daughter Elizabeth II inherited Sandringham as her private residence, and she has revelled in its country charm all her life. Throughout her reign the Queen and Prince Phillip spent two months every winter in Norfolk usually arriving by Royal train in early December, with the rest of the Royal family joining them to spend the Christmas period at Sandringham. The family celebrations usually commence with Christmas dinner and present-giving on Christmas Eve as a nod towards their German heritage, with the whole family, young and old, attending St. Mary Magdalene Church on Christmas morning. The Queen broadcast her first televised Christmas message from Sandringham in 1957. Her stay at Sandringham usually

Royal broadcast, Christmas 1934.

continues until mid-February, allowing her to commemorate the time of her father's death and her accession to the throne. As an ardent member of the Sandringham Women's Institute she also attends at least one meeting at Sandringham Village Hall. In February 1953, just a few weeks before her Coronation, she undertook one of her first Royal duties in visiting nearby Hunstanton, offering sympathy and comfort to those who had suffered in the disastrous East coast floods.

Sandringham Estate Today

Sandringham Estate today covers an area of 20,000 acres [8,100ha] incorporating several Norfolk villages; the largest are West Newton and Wolferton where 'The Royal Station' now hosts a small museum. Anmer, Babingley, Sandringham and Shernborne are picturesque estate hamlets, whilst Sandringham Country Park comprises 600 acres and together with the Sandringham Visitors' Centre is open to the general public throughout the year. In 1977, for her Silver Jubilee, the Queen opened Sandringham House to the public for the first time, and today visitors are welcomed through the summer months. The remainder of the estate lands and woodlands are either managed by estate workers or let to tenant farmers. There are several other properties on the estate including Anmer Hall, the residence of

Sandringham, 2011.

the Duke and Duchess of Cambridge, whilst York Cottage is now Sandringham's estate office. Wood Farm was home to Prince John until his short life ended in 1919, and when Prince Phillip [1921-2021] retired from Royal duties in 2017 he also lived there, until his short illness took him to London where he died in April 2021.

UNIQUE CHALK STREAMS SERVING UNIQUE CULTURAL TREASURES

As a means of exploring both the topography and rich cultural heritage of northwest Norfolk the visitor is urged to explore the many small rivers which originate and flow through the region. Lying along the banks of these waterways are any number of Norfolk's cultural treasures, where previous generations in creating this heritage had recognised the need for being in close proximity to water to sustain life and provide a means of communication. Later 17th and 18th century wealthy landowners, in pursuing the ideas of the English Landscape Movement of William Kent, Capability Brown and Norfolk's own Humphrey Repton [1752-1818] used these rivers to create lakes and watery landscapes offering superb views of this magnificent countryside from their large country houses.

As rare, spring-fed chalk streams these rivers sustain a unique and quite precious fauna and flora. There are only two hundred such waterways in the world and remarkably this region has at least nine of them, mostly flowing westwards to The Wash. Not surprisingly a whole host of nature reserves now lie alongside these chalk streams, characterised by being crystal clear and fast flowing. At least they should be, but over the ages many have been straightened and modified for drainage or flood defence purposes reducing their ecological diversity. The Norfolk Rivers Trust was created in 2011 with a remit to conserve and restore Norfolk rivers and wetland habitats, with much of their ongoing work focussed on these rare chalk streams.

River Stiffkey

The river Stiffkey largely forms the eastern border of northwest Norfolk running northwards from its source near Swanton Novers for some eighteen miles [29kms] out into the North Sea by the village of Stiffkey. Swanton comes from OE *Swana-tun,* the town of the swine herds, whilst Novers refers to Norman overlord Milo de Nuiers.

Rising in a small wooded lake, [TG 018329] which at 101 metres [331'] is one of the highest points in Norfolk, the stream passes close to Fulmodeston, then north through Thursford Wood Nature Reserve, where its 500-year old oaks are maintained by Norfolk Wildlife Trust. The river continues northwards between Thursford village, with its famous Thursford Steam Museum, and the curiously named Saxon villages of Little and Great Snoring. The name may come from '*the village of Snear's people*', or from Old English '*Sneare*' meaning 'swift', which may have been the original name for the river itself. Little Snoring church overlooks the river, with its ancient round tower separated from the remainder of the church, which presumably was built much later. Nearby is a memorial to all who served during WWII at RAF Little Snoring. Lying just past Little Snoring's Green Man pub on the A148 is NWT Brett's Wood Nature Reserve, an old conifer plantation teeming with woodland birds, but beware of picking fungi here as it is also the home of the highly poisonous Fly Agaric.

Little Snoring Airfield Memorial, 2021.

Turning south the river passes Thorpland Hall, a 16th century Tudor mansion with extensive gardens which are open to visitors on some summer weekends. Running northwest the river passes underneath the B1105 Fakenham to Wells road and into the grounds of East Barsham Manor. Dating from the 1520s, this magnificent Tudor hall with its pinnacled gatehouse was where Henry VIII and Anne Boleyn stayed when visiting the shrine at Walsingham. A 'prodigy house' built of expensive brick and comparable to Sutton Place, Surrey in style, it would have been the height of opulence in Henry's day, and still looks just as impressive today. It is privately owned.

Heading northwards through a deep valley, well, deep for Norfolk, the river passes Houghton St. Giles and its Slipper Chapel, don't miss the richly decorated rood screen in St. Giles Church. The National Roman Catholic Shrine is located about half a mile to the east close by the disused track of the Fakenham to Walsingham railway.

The largest village on the river's course is Little Walsingham, originally a Roman settlement and one of Europe's most important medieval pilgrimage sites; it is still an important religious centre today, especially at Easter. The limestone to build Walsingham Priory was carried by barge

Slipper Chapel (Basilica of St Mary), 2020.

around the coast from Northamptonshire and up the river Stiffkey, today only an imposing archway remains, gloriously surrounded in springtime by aconites and snowdrops. Visitors to the village, which includes the Priory Park, Slipper Chapel, Anglican Shrine and St. Mary's church, [*see Fonts of Distinction p. 30*], can reach here by rail on the restored Walsingham to Wells Light Railway.

North of Walsingham the river is joined by the Hindringham stream flowing from the east; its waters supply the moat and medieval fish pond of Hindringham Hall, a high-gabled manor house with splendid gardens open to the public in the summer. Flowing northwards through Wighton the river runs past two Bronze Age ring ditches, two Iron Age hillforts and perhaps a Roman temple, but little remains to be seen above ground today. Crossing water meadows the river soon skirts the edge of the circular embankments of Warham Iron Age fort, [*see Iron Age Forts p. 7*] where it is joined by another small tributary, the Binham stream on which lies Binham Priory. This was also dissolved by Henry VIII, but still retains its magnificent Priory church with an impressive font, all set amidst extensive flint cobble ruins.

Finally meandering through meadows alongside the coast road at Stiffkey [the name means 'stump island'] the river flows out to its estuary on Stiffkey Salt Marshes. Here is the home of the famous 'Stewkey Blues' cockles, where the shells of these creatures incorporate bands of bluey-grey silt. Armed with an old rake, a bucket and dressed in your oldest clothes a summer afternoon collecting cockles amidst the endless nodding heads of sea lavender and the shrill of sea birds can be a wonderfully captivating experience; but do check the tide table before venturing onto the marshes or the incoming flood tide rushing to fill unseen channels may be more captivating than you would like!

River Burn

Rising at the incongruously named Leicester Square [TF861342] in the parish of South Creake, the river Burn wends its 5 miles [8kms] course northwards to the sea at Burnham Overy Staithe through a series of villages which are some of the richest in Norfolk's cultural heritage.

St. Mary's, South Creake—font, 2021.

In South Creake village [from Welsh '*craig*', a rock] the stream is bordered by well-tended gardens and crossed by several quaint footbridges, from where it flows northwards past St. Mary's church. This enormous church hosts a whole squadron of carved angels in its roof, and a rare seven-sacrament font. A little to the south-east of the church is Bloodgate Iron Age Hill Fort, an open-access site now in the care of the Norfolk Archaeological Trust [*see Iron Age Forts p. 7*].

Northwards the river flows through the middle of North Creake and its manicured village green where you will find another St. Mary's church just as large as its counterpart down the road, with a monumental font cover and yet more angels.

St. Mary's, North Creake—roof, 2021.

Leaving the village the river flows across meadowland and through the ruins of Creake Abbey. Founded in 1217 as the Hospital of St. Bartholomew, when it embraced the rule of St. Augustine, the chapel became a Priory and subsequently an Abbey. Its demise came with a disastrous fire in 1484; much of the building was left derelict and an outbreak of plague killed most of the monks. By 1506, with the last Abbot dying alone, the lands were given to Christ's College, Cambridge. Today the open-access ruins are in the care of English Heritage, and here you will also find Creake Abbey Courtyard Shops and Café.

Creake Abbey, 2021.

Crossing open meadows to Burnham Thorpe the river passes into a small pool within a stone's throw of the site of the parsonage where Nelson was born, although sadly now long gone. All Saints Church holds much Nelson memorabilia including a copy of the great man's signature where he witnessed a marriage certificate, revealing somewhat surprisingly that his Christian name was Horace. The recently refurbished Lord Nelson pub was Nelson's local hostelry, although at the time he knew it as 'The Plough.'

Flowing past privately-owned Burnham Thorpe Manor the Burn feeds the moat of this flint and brick mostly 17th century grand house, although many of the distinctive cottages and farm buildings in this area are built of clunch, blocks

Cottage built using clunch, Burnham Overy Staithe, 2021.

Burnham Overy Staithe Watermill, 2021.

of particularly hard chalk. At Burnham Overy Town the river is often strengthened by Goose Beck, which intermittently flows through the middle of nearby Burnham Market. However, it seems that the force of the water often proved insufficient to drive the watermill built here in 1737, since a windmill was built onto the two-storey building in 1814, creating Union Mills, Burnham Overy Town. The mill was still in use in 1953 when it was flooded during the disastrous East Coast floods, but ceased working in 1969, and is now converted to private residences. The Norman church of St. Clement has a distinctive central tower between the nave and chancel, one of just fourteen such churches in Norfolk.

From the millpond the river passes through water meadows surrounding the magnificently preserved gatehouse and ruined walls of the 13th century Burnham Norton Carmelite Friary. Climb the outside staircase for wide views over the river valley and the ruined perimeter walls. The Friary is also in the care of the Norfolk Archaeological Trust and has open-access.

Within a couple of miles of the gatehouse the river enters Burnham Overy Lower Water Mill, located on a sharp bend in the A149 coast road just down the road from Burnham Overy Staithe and the Burnham Overy Tower Windmill. This was built in 1816 by Edmund Savory, who also owned the lower watermill and workers' cottages built in 1790. Both these and the tower mill are now owned by the National Trust and run as a unique holiday homes. The Flood Mark on the side of the building shows it was flooded to a depth of nine feet [2.7m] in the 1953 floods. Below the mill the river is banked with a sluice to prevent the ingress of seawater, and thence flows out to sea through Overy Marsh and Burnham Harbour. Now silted-up, the medieval port of Burnham Harbour [the name means '*homestead on a stream*'] is surrounded by seven parish churches; Burnham Norton, Overy, Ulph, Westgate, Sutton, Thorpe and Deepdale; all of which may be visited today, although Burnham Sutton is now in ruins.

River Tat

Sepecat Jaguar Gr 3 Jet, 2021.

Running south and eastwards from the chalk ridge the river Tat is a small but significant headwater tributary of the river Wensum, itself an important chalk stream which meanders its way right across central Norfolk to Norwich.

The Tat rises in NWT Syderstone Common Reserve, [TF 836315] barely four miles as the crow flies west of the river Stiffkey at East Barsham, but it flows in the opposite direction. The common is a site of special scientific interest [SSSI] hosting a colony of rare Natterjack toads. It lies just north of Tattersett [the name means '*Tathere's dwelling place*'] on the edge of the old RAF Sculthorpe airbase which is now used for military training. Here you will find on the village outskirts a reminder of Norfolk's important air defence role in WWII and the subsequent Cold War in the form of a Sepecat Jaguar Gr 3 Jet standing by a field for all to admire. Lovingly owned and restored by a local farmer, the plane forms part of the RAF Sculthorpe Heritage Centre collection, which is located nearby at Green Park Rural Centre, Chapel Street, Wicken Green, and is open to visitors on the first Sunday of the month from February-November. Just to the south of the airfield, off the A47 is Sculthorpe Moor Nature Reserve run by the Hawk and Owl Trust.

Passing under the A148 at Coxford, the crystal clear waters of the Tat once served Coxford Priory [or Broomsthorpe Priory], an Augustinian house initially founded around 1140 at St. Mary's church at East Rudham just up the road, but moved to Coxford by 1216. Dissolved in 1536 the ruins are visible from the road between Coxford and Broomsthorpe leading to Pynkney Hall, a mostly 17th century privately-owned large country house. Skirting Tatterford Common, a renowned bird-watching site, the Tat passes under a bridge on the Tatterford to Helhoughton road and broadens across a wooded valley, finally joining the Wensum just 4.5 miles [7.2km] from its source.

Venture a little further south from the bridge and the road crosses the old Fakenham to King's Lynn railway line at Raynham Park station, now carefully restored by its owners to celebrate the people who built and ran the old Midland and Great Northern railway [MGNR]. Beyond Helhoughton the river Wensum passes by Raynham Park and Hall [*see Turnip Townshend p. 10*] at East Raynham, whilst to the west is another WWII Bomber Command airfield, RAF West Raynham,

Raynham Park station, 2021.

and just a couple of miles further west is its satellite base RAF Great Massingham. The latter is now farmland but RAF West Raynham remained operational until the 1990s and was converted to a Business Park in 2007. Visitors will find a memorial to all those who served on the base, and also its privately owned restored Control Tower which is open to visitors for special events.

River Hun

The tiny river Hun rises in the extensive grounds of Hunstanton Park [TF695408] and flows northwards for a mere four miles [6.3kms] to the North Sea near Holme-next-the-Sea.

Hunstanton Hall, the seat of the Le Strange family, is a country house dating from the 15th century with many additions and alterations; it now comprises privately-owned apartments. The author P.G. Wodehouse was a frequent visitor in the 1930s, perhaps his fictional Blandings Castle is modelled on Hunstanton Hall.

Emerging from the park the Hun meanders around the back of Old Hunstanton, [don't miss the RNLI Lifeboat Visitor Centre] and dissipates in the wide marshes of Holme Dunes Nature Reserve managed by Norfolk Wildlife Trust. Located on the very top left hand corner of Norfolk, NWT Holme Dunes Reserve is renowned for often attracting rare species of migrant birds. Holme Beach was also the site of Seahenge, an enigmatic Bronze Age circle [*see Seahenge p. 6*].

Heacham River

The Heacham rises in remote fields [TF762339] a little to the north of Bircham Windmill, a working mill, bakery and pleasant watering hole for a weary traveller. It flows in a north-westerly direction towards the sea for some ten miles [16.4kms] until its outfall into The Wash at Heacham Beach.

From the windmill you can see the cranes of the Construction Industry Training Centre based on the former RAF Bircham Newton, initially laid out during WWI, later operating as part of Coastal Command during WWII and the Cold War. Nearby, a ruined church tower stands lonely in a field at Bircham Tofts, one of the meanings of '*toft*' is '*a deserted site.*'

The first real evidence of the Heacham comes in the centre of Fring [perhaps '*Frea's people*'] by the church, a delightful spot where from a long lake the river passes under the bridge in a 'Constable' scene which is only missing a hay wain. The river is crossed by the Peddars Way running through open countryside in a north-westerly direction. It then enters a shallow wooded valley passing through the 1200 acre Sedgeford Hall Estate [*see The Sedgeford Hoard p. 7*] The hall is a large mid-18th century L-shaped country house where today you can hire the west wing as a classy holiday home for fifteen people, or the whole place with nineteen bedrooms for forty! It then passes under a bridge by Sedgeford village green near the church.

Bircham Windmill, 2021.

Crossing under the B1454 the Heacham turns west towards the only water mill on the river. Heacham's Caley Mill stands on a medieval site but the present structure was built in 1840 of carrstone in a Gothic style. Originally used to grind corn, the mill has been used for lavender production since 1932 when the Norfolk Lavender company developed some hundred acres of the surrounding poor sandy drylands, ideally suited to grow the highly scented herb. They offer tours and produce a wide range of lavender oil products, not only the usual toiletries but also jams and marmalades. This author's best tip for culinary lavender is to add a few sprigs to the rosemary and fennel that you use to stuff a sea bass or bream for roasting on the barbecue.

Now demolished Heacham Hall was the seat of the Rolfe family; one of its most famous sons John Rolfe [1585-1622] was a merchant venturer and one of the early English settlers of North America. He successfully grew tobacco at the Jamestown colony, where he married Lady Rebecca Rolfe in 1614, but today we know her better as Pocahontas. John, Rebecca and their young son returned to England in 1615 where the family were received at Court, but as they were preparing to return to America Rebecca died; she is buried in Gravesend church. The story of Pocahontas is commemorated on Heacham's village sign, located where the river passes under the A149 coast road. It then flows through Heacham village under small bridges and into Heacham Park, where the river feeds a small lake and visitors feed the many waterside ducks.

After the lake the river is joined by a small tributary flowing intermittently from the north at Ringstead Downs, a Norfolk Wildlife Trust nature reserve set in a steep sided often dry valley of chalk grassland. An SSSI, this species-rich site hosts many butterflies, yellowhammers, whitethroats, linnets and rare chalkland plants including Common Rock Rose with its strongly scented lemon-yellow flowers.

Crossing low level meadows the river turns south running parallel with the coast

Caley Mill—Norfolk Lavender, 2021.

through Heacham's small holiday resort with the old restored railway station and at North Beach a memorial to the people drowned here in the 1953 floods. The river then flows towards South Beach and into a series of pools which discharge at low tide through tidal flaps. Now land-locked, these pools were once Heacham Harbour where remains of old timber jetties can still be seen poking above the water. The river finally ends in coastal dunes just by Shepherd's Port caravan site.

River Ingol

The river Ingol rises a little to the west of Shernborne in a marshy valley [TF 712323] and runs a mere six miles [10kms] to The Wash at Wolferton Creek. Flowing westward across agricultural land towards Snettisham, the river must have got its name from the hamlet of Ingoldisthorpe lying just to the north. Here is a Viking village dating from around the 9th century named from an Old Norse warrior '*Ingiald*', who may well have sailed his longboat up the Ingol to settle here. Scandinavian weights have been discovered by metal detectorists nearby. The second part of the name, 'thorpe', is also Viking and means a smaller village near a larger one, though this larger settlement has now been lost. However, a very rare Thor's Hammer Pendant has been discovered near Hillington by the river Babingley, suggesting this river may have also given access for a Viking settlement.

Recognising the importance of the Ingol as a rare chalk stream, in 2018 an innovative new wetland was constructed in marshes next to the traditional Ingoldisthorpe Sewage Treatment Plant. A series of settling ponds planted with carefully selected native aquatic plants now provide a natural, low-cost sustainable water filtration method to considerably improve the water quality. Undertaken with the guidance of the Norfolk Wetlands Trust, this ground-breaking site is often open to visitors.

Downriver at Snettisham stands a watermill, built of local Carrstone in 1800 on the site of an earlier mill. In Domesday times there were seven mills at Snettisham, more than anywhere else in the country. Restored and brought back to working order in the 1980s and now run as a holiday home, the mill sits in an acre of grounds which include a lakeside garden, river and sluice race. Snettisham church with its landmark spire overlooks the river marshes, whilst Snettisham Park Farm on the outskirts of the village is a working farm and popular visitor attraction, especially during the lambing season.

From Snettisham the lowermost reaches of the river run parallel to the coastline, backing up at high tide into a series of ponds with tidal flaps discharging into the sea at low tide. These coastal mudflats and marshes, all part of the RSPB Snettisham Nature Reserve, host tens of thousands of wading birds when spring tides push them off their feeding grounds in The Wash.

Snettisham church with its landmark spire, 2021.

Babingley River

Rising at the base of a steep chalk scarp face just west of ruined Flitcham Abbey (or St. Mary's Priory) [TF744264], the Babingley river runs for some twelve miles [19.6kms] to the river Great Ouse at Wootton Marshes.

Flitcham Abbey was an Augustinian Priory founded in 1217 as a dependent cell of Walsingham Priory. Dissolved in 1538, the site is now Flitcham Abbey Farm, one of the many tenanted farms of the Sandringham Estate. Run on environmentally sustainable lines, the farm hosts a public bird hide which overlooks the meandering river, but little can be seen of the old Abbey.

Running south westwards the river passes into Hillington Hall Park under a bridge and large gatehouse, but venture further south onto the main road where there is a larger, more impressive gatehouse built as a reconstruction of King's Lynn's East Gate. Next door in the fields behind the pub, a local nursery organises springtime tours of their colourful tulip fields bordering the river, raising funds for a local hospice.

The Babingley skirts the southern edge of Sandringham Estate and flows under the A149 King's Lynn to Hunstanton road by Castle Rising. This medieval fortification was built soon after 1138 by Norman knight William d'Aubigny as a combination fortress and palatial hunting lodge for the surrounding deer park. The castle was later sold to Queen Isabella, dubbed the She-Wolf of France and mother of Edward III. Henry VIII sold off Castle Rising, which is now in the care of English Heritage. Nearby is the Trinity Hospital, an alms-house founded by Henry Howard between 1609 and 1614 providing sheltered accommodation for twelve elderly '*sisters*' of an '*honest life and conversation*'. Even today the current residents, dressed in their traditional tall black hats and red capes bearing the

Howard badge, cross the road every Sunday to attend St. Lawrence's Church to pray for their founder.

Heading northwards the river passes under Babingley Bridge to its namesake village, [the name means '*the meadow of Babba's people*']. Another deserted village, Babingley today comprises just a row of estate houses on the busy A149 main road and a 'tin tabernacle' dedicated to SS Mary and Felix dating from the 1880s. In the marshes opposite, the medieval church ruins of St. Felix lie on private lands at Church Hall Farm. By tradition St. Felix of Burgundy is said to have landed in Britain around 630 AD to introduce Christianity to East Anglia. His ship was wrecked in a storm and sought refuge in the Babingley river. According to legend he was rescued by beavers, and subsequently made one of the creatures a bishop. Babingley's village sign by the row of cottages uniquely records the tradition.

Babingley's village sign, 2021.

Just a little to the north of the village, in 2019 some 4000 acres of arable land and woodland at Ken Hill Farm was turned over to a major rewilding project. Intended to tackle climate change and improve air and water quality, one of their principal changes includes the re-introduction of the Eurasian beaver into a fifty acre enclosure.

The Babingley completes its journey meandering northwards towards The Wash through coastal fen and marshland, but is then captured by a man-made channel that takes it southward through Wootton Marsh where it outpours into the Great Ouse estuary at Lynn Channel.

River Cong

The river Cong, a tiny 1½ mile [2.4km] tributary of the Babingley, rises in the hundred acre grounds of Congham Lodge [TF 721239]. The Lodge is a listed Great House, built around 1800 on the site of an old water mill, enigmatically described on Faden's map as an 'oil mill'. Flowing over an impressive waterfall, the water power may have pressed rape seed oil or perhaps produced bonemeal, as whalebones have been found in the grounds. The Lodge is now privately owned but run as an upmarket B&B establishment. The Cong flows under the A148 [King's Lynn to Fakenham Road] and joins the Babingley close by Gatton Water Caravan park.

Gaywood River

The Gaywood river, sometimes known as the river Gay, is a tributary of the Great Ouse, rising in Derby Fen between Grimston and Gayton near Well Hall [TF726203] flowing for seven miles [11kms] westward where it joins the main river in King's Lynn.

Derby Fen is a remnant of a valley fen system; its underlying sandstone geology means that whilst the Gaywood is a spring-fed chalk stream, the surrounding fen comprises damp acidic grasslands supporting a unique heathland flora. Designated by Norfolk Wildlife Trust as the Gaywood Valley Living Landscape there are two adjacent reserves here, NWT Roydon Common and Tony Hallat Memorial Reserve hosting rare species including the Black Darter dragonfly, the Raft Spider and Sundew carnivorous plant.

Evidence of a Roman settlement at Well Hall has been recognised with the discovery over several decades of building scatter, high quality pottery and coins. This is also a scheduled medieval settlement site of subtle earthworks, they may represent a small priory founded here as a cell of St. Stephen's Abbey, Caen. Only ever comprising a small manor house, farmstead and a mill occupied by a few monks, as an alien priory it was seized by the Crown in the 14th century during Edward III's wars with France.

From Derby Fen the stream runs under Leziate Drove, [Leziate means 'a gate in a meadow'] along the southern edge of Sugar Fen and westwards into open countryside skirting to the north of Bawsey village, Leziate Sand quarry and the medieval ruins of St. James' church. Starkly silhouetted on a small hill, the church is unusually constructed of carrstone and iron conglomerate, with some flint and limestone dressings. In 1999 a Time Team dig found a 14th century tile and a skeleton here, where the skull had sustained a powerful sword blow. The site may have been Saxon in origin and raided by 9th century Vikings.

Passing under the A149 King's Lynn to Hunstanton road the river has been heavily modified by flood defence works, and enters the urban Gaywood area of King's Lynn. The top of Kettlewell Lane was the site of the former Kettle Mill, where a 15th century horse-powered mill drew drinking water from the river in kettle-like containers, discharging the water into elm conduits. Heading south by the railway station the river curls through gardens and parkland at 'The Walks' close by remnants of the town wall, finally entering a culvert at Millfleet and Stonegate Street and discharging into the Great Ouse.

River Nar

The Nar rises on a high plateau of lightly wooded open farmland near Mileham [TF 896198] and flows westward for fifteen miles [24kms] to its outfall into the river Great Ouse, just to the south of King's Lynn. A significant trout stream for most of its length, in its lower reaches this river also supports migratory sea trout. The Nar Valley Way footpath follows the course of the river from Litcham to King's Lynn crossing the Peddars Way National Trail at Castle Acre.

Lying in the triangle of the villages of Litcham, Tittleshall and Mileham, the river source is just a mile from the open-access earthwork remains of the Norman early 12th century motte and bailey Mileham Castle. Lying next to the B1145 road the castle meadows are accessed through a kissing gate opposite Burwood Hall's gateway.

At 63mOD Tittleshall lies on the high watershed between the river Wensum, which flows eastward to Norwich, and the Nar flowing westward to King's Lynn, with the remains of the deserted village of Godwick nearby. This is also an open-access site of extensive earthworks and a ruined church tower with a trail tracing the old village. English Heritage interpretation panels guide visitors over the grassy slopes. Godwick Hall is a working farm and also provides a wedding venue in its barn set in expansive grasslands.

Initially flowing east and then south, the Nar flows under the B1145 Litcham road and turning westwards enters a series of lakes at Lexham Hall, a large Grade I listed mansion built around 1700. Today it is privately owned, the estate lets shooting rights and the gardens are open for charity five times a year. Here you will also find the round-towered Saxon church of St. Andrew's East Lexham by the enormous barn of Lexham Hall Farm. Meandering westwards the river reaches the lakes of West Lexham Manor, now run as an eco-friendly accommodation and

Castle Acre, 2013.

events centre with various festivals held throughout the year. Crossing under the A1065 Swaffham to Fakenham road, the river runs to the south of Castle Acre, [the name means '*cultivated land*'] passing the ruins of the Norman castle and Priory. Both were founded soon after the Conquest by William de Warenne; in the late 11th century Castle Acre played an important role in the affairs of state with many visits from royalty. Even today the village still demonstrates one of the finest examples of Norman town planning found anywhere in the country. With its extensive motte and bailey castle earthworks, ruined Priory buildings, remnants of fortified walls and Bailey gatehouse, any visitor strolling through Castle Acre will truly find a sense of walking through the pages of history. Castle Acre Priory ruins, now in the care of English Heritage lie on the north side of the valley looming above the river, where a deep ford provides a delightful spot to appreciate the weed strewn fast-flowing water teeming with darting trout.

From Castle Acre the river widens and meanders westwards past South Acre Hall to West Acre Priory. The village green just by the church, with its war memorial, village sign and imposing gateway to the Priory presents a quintessentially English scene, where All Saints' church clock exhorts the visitor to 'WATCH AND PRAY' in place of the usual twelve numerals. A keen-eyed geologist will also observe that the cottages on one side of the road are built of flint, but on the other side of gingery carrstone, giving a clue to the underlying geological boundary between Lower Cretaceous sandstone and Middle Cretaceous chalk. The Priory was founded in 1100 by the de Toni family and dissolved in 1538. Today the ruins provide an emotive setting for a host of music and arts events, whilst the West Acre Theatre, housed in the nearby former Primitive Methodist chapel, is a theatre, cinema and arts workshop hosting a full range of summer events.

West Acre Priory gatehouse, 2021.

Flowing ever westwards the waters of the Nar have been extensively widened into a series of lakes providing an opulent vista from Narford Hall, one of the most imposing, but least known 18th century grand houses in Norfolk. Privately owned, the hall today is home to the Fairfax & Favor fashion brand. As the river approaches Narborough it passes a wooded plantation which hides Narborough Iron Age Fort [*see Iron Age Forts p. 7*].

Reaching Narborough the Nar passes under the modern A47 bypass, but head for the old main road in the middle of the village where there is ample evidence of 18th century engineering works, when the river was made navigable from its mouth to West Acre by an Act of Parliament passed in 1751. Ten single-gate sluices and a pound lock were used to handle the changes in level. Today the sluices by the old Narborough watermill and maltings are equipped with fish ladders to assist migratory sea trout to reach their spawning grounds upriver. Narborough Hall, yet another imposing country house dating to the 16th century, probably built from one or more of the surrounding dissolved monasteries, is set in seventy-nine acres of park, with two lakes and a stretch of the river Nar. Its open gardens are today used as an arts and wedding venue; Narborough Trout Fishery is nearby as is a small car park on Chalk Lane which gives access to NWT Narborough Railway Line Reserve. This disused railway embankment is a rare chalk grassland habitat hosting orchids, marsh helleborine and autumn gentian, with over thirty species of butterflies recorded here.

Narford Hall, 2021.

Narborough old mill and Malthouse, 2021.

A mile downstream from Narborough village the Nar Valley Way passes the Old Whalebone Mill on the opposite bank. The recently restored large waterwheel stands in proud testament to the region's industrial and agricultural past; it can be seen turning on special open days. Whalebone from King's Lynn's traditional whaling industry was brought here by river for grinding into bonemeal for fertiliser, which was then shipped back by barge to King's Lynn port for further shipment. Local slaughterhouses also provided raw material, there is even a gruesome record that exhumed human remains from cemeteries in Hamburg were shipped to King's Lynn and on to Narborough for processing.

From here the valley opens into a wide marshy landscape, but the river is contained in long canal stretches as a result of the navigation works. It passes Pentney Abbey, yet another 12th century monastic ruin where the impressive gatehouse, barn and grounds are now yet another wedding venue. Nearby are large sand and gravel works and the valley is peppered with lakes reclaimed from the workings. NWT East Winch Common Nature Reserve lies on the northern flank of the valley, an area of mixed heather, wet heath and ponds, home to a number of interesting plants and invertebrates.

Turning north the river channel runs alongside the Great Ouse, passing the site of the old whale blubber works, finally outpouring through a sluice into the Great Ouse in South Lynn.

Pentney Abbey gatehouse, 2021.

THE CHURCHES OF NORTHWEST NORFOLK

Just as in the rest of Norfolk, the northwest region boasts a remarkable collection of some ninety five medieval churches, including at least fifteen with distinctive round towers. Just about every one either contains a treasure, or is a treasure in itself, offering every sort of joy to a dedicated 'church basher.' Here are some of the 'not to be missed', starting with a few examples that are all too easily missed.

Lost But Not Forgotten

Sadly, the region is well blessed with deserted medieval villages and their often ruined churches, including Godwick, Egmere, Waterden, Quarles, Great Barwick, Burnham Sutton, Hempton, Pudding Norton, Bircham Tofts, Babingley and Pensthorpe. The reasons for a village being deserted are often complex, but the disastrous loss of population during the Black Death and the resultant move by landowners from arable crops to pasture account for many desertions.

Lying just west of Walsingham, the 12th century St. Edmund's church Egmere had only five parishioners in 1523, by 1603 there was only one household and the church had become a barn. The ruined tower surrounded by earthworks is visible from the North Creake to South Creake road. Egmere means '*Ecga's pond*', whilst another deserted medieval village, Waterden, where the name means '*valley with a pond*' lies just two miles away. The ancient trackways surrounding Waterden Farm are lined by distinctive earthworks of rectangular cottages and a large enclosure where the Hall, demolished in 1781, was situated.

Quarles, the name may refer to a nearby but as yet unidentified prehistoric stone circle, was abandoned by 1571, only a picturesque ruined wall of the church remains. This tiny hamlet lies directly south of the Holkham Estate. St. Mary Great Barwick, just east of Docking, was also abandoned in the 16th century; remnants of the church are to be found in Churchyard Plantation.

St. Ethelbert's Burnham Sutton has metre-high ruins now carefully maintained by the Burnham Market Society, whilst Holy Trinity, Hempton is perhaps the least known of Norfolk's lost churches, and one of the most difficult to find. Tucked away in a southern suburb of Fakenham down a lane past the Memorial Hall, from the outside the church looks Victorian, but this sideways extension hides a 14th century chancel arch. To complicate things further a 1950's westward extension was constructed from the demolished masonry of the church of St. Michael-at-Thorn in Norwich, badly damaged in WWII.

From Hempton a ten-minute walk down Dereham Road will take you to the curiously-shaped ruined tower of St. Margaret Pudding Norton, with its 12th century carrstone quoins below and 13th century limestone blocks above. The village was deserted during the reign of Elizabeth I when the local landowner turned out the inhabitants to make way for grazing. Norton simply means a village north of another, but the meaning of Pudding remains obscure.

Four miles west is yet another deserted medieval village at Pensthorpe, with remnants of the church built into the Manor Farm buildings. The earthworks of the lost village and moat are visible on aerial photos, but much of the old village has been damaged by gravel quarrying. Today, these flooded workings are incorporated in Pensthorpe Natural Park, a multi-faceted wetland visitor attraction lying on the river Wensum.

Precious Saxon Remains

The deserted village of Houghton-on-the-Hill, lying just south east of Swaffham, today only comprises a farm and St. Mary's church, tucked away amongst trees up a lonely farm track. Lying in ruins, the church was rescued in the 1990s by retired engineer Bob Davey MBE, [1929-2021] when his tireless restoration work revealed Saxon wall paintings dating from the time of the Domesday Book; the earliest-known example of large-system wall paintings in the country.

Set on a distinctive circular mound close by the river Nar the church of St. Andrew's East Lexham may have been built on an early pagan site subsequently adopted by Christianity. Crudely built of flints and mortar, the Saxon round tower of the church is thought to be the oldest in England, constructed around 900AD. Inside the visitor will find a rare mixture of Saxon and early English architecture combined with striking 21st century artworks. Just down the road at West Lexham stands St. Nicholas church with another late Saxon round tower, although the remainder of the church was rebuilt in the 1880s.

St Mary's, Houghton-on-the-Hill, 2012.

Lying a little to the southeast of the Lexhams, St. Andrew's Great Dunham is an almost entirely Saxon church with its central square tower set between the nave and chancel. The chancel and porch are 15th century but the tower and church are all pre-Conquest, don't miss the distinctive triangular- headed doorway at the west end of the nave.

Also with a central tower is All Saints' church Newton-by-Castle Acre. This Saxon church was once cruciform in shape, but the transepts forming the arms of the cross have now disappeared. Much of the architecture is late Saxon, simple in construction with brick floors and white walls, offering the visitor a sanctuary of calm from the busy Swaffham to Fakenham road just outside. Undoubtedly this ancient church offered a similar sanctuary to the many pilgrims who plodded this road on their way to the shrine at Walsingham.

Fonts of Distinction

There are around forty churches across East Anglia with rare seven-sacrament fonts, and northwest Norfolk boasts four of them at South Creake, Binham Priory, Gayton Thorpe and Little Walsingham. Usually octagonal, seven of the faces of these pre-Reformation stone fonts are carved with scenes portraying the Catholic religious milestones of a person's life and faith; Baptism, Confirmation, Confession, Matrimony, Holy Orders, Celebrating Mass and Last Rites. The eighth panel often portrays Christ's Crucifixion. Undoubtedly the font at St. Mary Little Walsingham is the finest in the country, set on two enormous stone plinths and superbly carved on every face. A disastrous fire destroyed much of this church in 1961 but the font survived and the church has now been carefully rebuilt protecting this medieval treasure of '*England's Nazareth*'.

The unique square Norman font at St. Mary's Burnham Norton, a round tower church just down the road from Brancaster Roman Fort, pursues a different theme. The sides of the font depict farming life through the changing seasons, a fitting tribute for this important agricultural region.

Detail on the Little Walsingham font, 2021.

The late medieval font at St. Mary's Church, Docking is yet another shining example of the stonemason's art, where the panels show the twelve apostles. But it is the stem of this chalice-shaped font which portrays eight female helper-saints; all venerated in the pre-Reformation church for their ability to aid the faithful to meet the ardours of life, and especially childbirth. Indeed, three of the figures are seated holding babies, the Blessed

Virgin and child, St. Anne holding the infant Virgin and St. Elizabeth with the infant St. John the Baptist.

A last word on fonts; to the medieval parishioners they were the most vulnerable, potentially dangerous parts of the church. For here was where the devil could be lurking intent on taking the souls of innocents who were yet to receive the protection afforded by Christian baptism. For this reason it is often worth looking carefully at the masonry surrounding the font to discover medieval graffiti. These symbols were scratched by ordinary churchgoers to ward off evil; a devil pinned down with nails or pentagular stars are typical. A careful search in the church of St. Mary the Virgin Sedgeford will reveal many such symbols but they are hard to spot; a small LED torch giving a glancing light often helps.

More Like Cathedrals

Swaffham's impressive market place with its 18th century Market Cross also holds the town sign with its picture of John Chapman, the legendary Pedlar of Swaffham. He had a dream that he would find his fortune on London Bridge, so he went to London where a sceptical shopkeeper related his own dream of treasure hidden under a tree in the market place of a town in Norfolk called Swaffham: and it proved to be true! Looming over the eastern side of the market place is the massive 15th century church of St. Peter and St. Paul with its vast hammer beam roof, and of course a carving of both the Pedlar and his dog are found on the ends of the front pews. As church warden, in 1462 John Chapman paid for the north aisle, south porch and much more beside to embellish this magnificent church. The Swaffham place name means '*homestead of the Swabians*'; these Anglo-Saxon people from southwest Germany are thought to be some of the earliest invaders of Britain.

St. Margaret's Minster, King's Lynn stands on the Saturday Market Place, more of a small cathedral rather than just a parish church. This magnificent 15th century edifice has everything, two imposing towers, soaring pillars, a splendid 13th century chancel, a galleried clerestory and two of the largest and most elaborate brasses in England. Don't miss the assemblage of flood marks in the porch showing that the church has been flooded numerable times. Head across town to the Tuesday Market Place and at the western end stands lofty 13th century St. Nicholas Chapel, where having been rebuilt in 1420 you will find yet more medieval splendour in polished oak, brass and stone. Both these churches were built by the town's wealthy merchants intent on saving their souls, with many of them buried in St. Nicholas chapel. Look carefully at the mural monuments and ledger stones and here you will find Sir Benjamin Keene [1697-1757] and former King's Lynn mayor Richard Clarke. You will also find gravestones of the Cruso family, including a couple of Robinsons; names recorded by Daniel Defoe when he visited King's Lynn in 1724 and used by him for the tale of his eponymous twice-shipwrecked hero.

Heading westwards to the far reaches of the region the visitor will find even more large and magnificent Marshland churches. Light and airy St. Mary's Church West Walton has a separate lofty bell tower, and here you will also find a flood board recording '*be it kept in perpetuall Memory that on yᵉ first of November 1613 the Sea broke in and overflowed all Marshland, to the grate danger of Mens lives, and losse of goods.*' Terrington St. Clement's church has long been dubbed '*the Cathedral of the marshes*' given that it is fifty one metres [167 ft] long and it too has a separate bell tower. Undoubtedly these high towers were used by the parishioners as a safe refuge whenever the angry sea came crashing across the marshes.

PEOPLE AND PLACES

Given northwest Norfolk's prosperity over many centuries it is not surprising that the people of the region gained renown on a national and international stage. Here are a few of the most noteworthy who have left their indelible mark on the region, although few are buried in their homeland.

A Fleet of Admirals and Explorers

Visitors crossing the county boundary will find a signpost proudly proclaiming that Norfolk is 'Nelson's county', with the church at his birthplace at Burnham Thorpe in northwest Norfolk holding much memorabilia of the great naval commander. But 1st Viscount Horatio Lord Nelson [1758-1805] joined an impressive line of seafarers from that small corner of Norfolk, with three 17th century Admirals of the Fleet all born within a few short miles of the Burnhams. Sir Cloudesley Shovell [1650-1707] and Rear Admiral Sir John Narbrough [1640-1688] both came from Cockthorpe, a tiny hamlet just a few minutes' drive from Wells, whilst Vice Admiral Sir Christopher Myngs [1625-1666] hailed from nearby Salthouse. By a remarkable coincidence, in the 1660s Myngs was the captain, Narbrough the lieutenant and Shovell the lowly cabin boy, all serving in the same ship.

Christopher Myngs was an archetypal 'Elizabethan' buccaneer making repeated attacks in the 1650s on the Spanish Main out in the West Indies. Not averse to diverting some of this captured state-owned treasure to his own pocket, he was returned to England under a cloud, but distinguished himself in the Four Day Battle of the second Anglo-Dutch wars. Having been seriously wounded in the face he fought on, but a few days later died of his wounds in London and is buried in a lost grave in a small park in Whitechapel, east London.

John Narbrough also fought the Anglo-Dutch wars but came to prominence as an explorer and navigator, voyaging in the 1690s into the Pacific Ocean and along the coast of what is now modern day Chile. His illustrated journals of the flora and fauna of South America, and his accurate depictions of its harbours now lie in the British Library available for all to admire. He is buried in St. Clement's church Dover.

Cloudesley Shovell, the son of a yeoman farmer joined the Royal Navy as a boy and by 1676 gained renown by burning four ships lying just under the castle walls of the Dey of Tripoli. He went on to greater renown in the reign of William and Mary becoming the leading fighting admiral of his age, but disaster was close at hand. In 1707 returning from a successful campaign fighting the French fleet at Toulon, four ships of his fleet foundered on the rocks of the Scilly Isles. Two thousand men drowned. Shovell got on shore only, it is claimed, to be murdered for his emerald signet ring. He is buried in Westminster Abbey.

Born in King's Lynn, George Vancouver [1757-1798] won renown as one of this country's most accomplished explorer-navigators. As a boy Vancouver sailed with Captain Cook, later exploring the southwest coast of Australia. But his greatest success came in exploring the west coast of Canada and North America and the island that bears his name. Today he is poorly remembered, but his statue stands proudly on the Custom House Quay in the town of his birth, and he is buried in St. Peter's Church, Petersham, Richmond-on-Thames.

Sir Cloudesley Shovell.

A protégé of Nelson, Baronet William Hoste [1780-1828] was born at Godwick Hall, Tittleshall and, like Nelson, attended Paston School in North Walsham. He joined the great man on the '*Agamemnon*' and was at Tenerife when Nelson lost his right arm. In March 1811 Captain Hoste made his name by claiming victory when vastly outnumbered by the French in the Battle of Lisa in the Adriatic. He was a member of the committee which set up the Norfolk Naval Pillar in Gt. Yarmouth as a memorial to Nelson. He died of tuberculosis in 1828 and is buried in St. John's Chapel, London.

To date there is no satisfactory explanation as to why this small corner of Norfolk produced quite so many naval heroes, but several of them were distantly related. Although all born in northwest Norfolk, none of them are laid to rest in the county of their birth.

There are however two famous mariners who are buried in Norfolk. The Langham farmer Captain Frederick Marriot CB FRS [1792-1848] was a naval officer who served with distinction. He also invented a lifeboat, was a keen zoologist and a successful author writing two highly acclaimed books, '*Mr. Midshipman Easy*' and '*Children of the New Forest*'. He is buried under a circular stone obelisk in Langham Churchyard.

Richard Woodget [1847-1928] was born at Burnham Norton and became the most famous captain of the clipper ship '*Cutty Sark*'. He inspired his crew to great effect, regularly making the return voyage to Australia in record time, with many of his protégés going on to great things in their later naval careers. In retirement Captain Woodget supported the Shipwrecked Fishermen and Mariners Royal Benevolent Society, who in turn placed the memorial stone anchor on his grave in Burnham Norton churchyard.

King's Lynn's Women of Courage

Margery Kempe nee Burnham [c.1373-c.1440] was a medieval mystic born in King's Lynn; her '*Book of Margery Kempe*' is credited with being the first known autobiography in English literature; and what a life she led! She was married to brewer John Kempe and they had fourteen children. After the birth of her first child Margery had many visions, which convinced her that she had a '*great intimacy with Christ*' and should undertake in 1414 a pilgrimage to Jerusalem. She wandered through Europe and the Holy Land weeping and sobbing so vehemently that many shunned her, thinking she was possessed by the devil. On her return to England she dictated her remarkable story in English rather than Latin or French; constantly referring to herself as 'this creature'. Preserved by a Catholic family over generations, her work is now recognised as an exceptional story of religious experience and a unique social history of medieval life.

The Wells-next-the-Sea parish register for December 1583 records that fourteen fishermen, '*perished upon ye west coast ....whose deaths were brought to pass by the detestable working of an excrable witch of King's Lynn whose name was Mother Gabley....*' Evidently she did this by '*the boiling or rather labouring of certain eggs in a pail full of cold water.*' There was sufficient evidence for the poor soul to be brought to trial, however her ultimate fate is unknown, but what a harsh judgement inflicted on her just because the men were unfortunately caught in a storm.

Just before Mistress Mary Smith was hanged (some say boiled alive) for witchcraft in the Tuesday Market Place, King's Lynn on January 12th 1616, she predicted that her heart would burst from her body and fly above the window of the magistrate's house who convicted her. Go there today and you will find a lozenge-shaped recess cut into the brickwork of No. 15, within which is the shape of a heart. Whether this is an actual imprint of Mary's heart, or a later interpretation of the incident, is unclear. Certainly the age of the building is much later than the seventeenth century, but you must visit and decide for yourself.

The Talented Carters of Swaffham

As the son of Samuel Carter, a notable Victorian animal artist, Howard Carter [1874-1939] was brought up in Swaffham by two of his aunts, although both his parents were Swaffham-born. Howard inherited his father's artistic skills and an abiding passion in Egyptology from his visits to the collections at nearby Didlington Hall, the home of Lord Amherst of Hackney. So it comes as no surprise that Howard Carter became a brilliant archaeologist, with his greatest discovery made in 1922 of the tomb of Tutankhamun. His sister Amy was an accomplished miniaturist; brother Verney an engraver, whilst another brother William was a portrait painter and Royal Academician.

As a distant cousin of Howard, art and woodwork teacher Harry Carter [1907-1983] was brought up in Swaffham and taught at Hammond's Grammar school there for thirty years. Harry's artworks are found in every corner of Norfolk, for it was he who made, or inspired others to make, the hundreds of village signs which grace the Norfolk countryside. Harry's first sign was of course the Pedlar of Swaffham, and following Royal consent being granted in 1953 for a sign at Anmer to celebrate the Coronation, Harry's talents were in great demand. Often with the help of his students he made dozens of others, charging little for his efforts. Sign-making was his abiding hobby, and of course it is his abiding legacy.

CONCLUSION

With its productive farmland, busy ports, coastal resorts, wild coastline, charming villages and unique waterways; across the millennia northwest Norfolk has proved to be most attractive to many different people, for many different reasons. For the most part these people prospered from their time in this region, enhancing the economic fortunes of this country, and enabling the creation of a remarkable cultural heritage as rich and varied as anywhere else in the British Isles. The region's gently rolling countryside saw the creation of important defensive sites ranging from Iron Age Forts, a Roman Shorefort, medieval fortifications in King's Lynn and many WWII airfields, all strategically placed to defend the region and the nation in its hour of need. Important monastic centres sprang up in medieval times, only to be abandoned and often re-purposed into local churches, grand houses and civic buildings. In turn these sites in themselves are now heritage treasures, liberally sprinkled across the region. The 20th century saw the creation of many 'green tourism' nature reserves, with 21st century re-wilding projects now creating even more. So it is not surprising that this part of Norfolk sees some half a million staying visitors and eight million day visitors every year; all intent on enjoying this green and very pleasant land.

Index